A Kid's Guide to
GENEALOGY

USING TECHNOLOGY TO FIND YOUR
FAMILY HISTORY

Tammy Gagne

Mitchell Lane
PUBLISHERS

P.O. Box 196
Hockessin, Delaware 19707

Mitchell Lane
PUBLISHERS

Basic Genealogy for Kids
How to Research Your Ancestry
Using Technology to Find Your Family History
Design Your Family Tree

Copyright © 2012 by Mitchell Lane Publishers

Printing   1   2   3   4   5   6   7   8   9

PUBLISHER'S NOTE: The facts on which this book is based have been thoroughly researched. Documentation of such research can be found on page 44. While every possible effort has been made to ensure accuracy, the publisher will not assume liability for damages caused by inaccuracies in the data, and makes no warranty on the accuracy of the information contained herein.

The Internet sites referenced herein were active as of the publication date. Due to the fleeting nature of some web sites, we cannot guarantee that they will all be active when you are reading this book.

**Library of Congress
Cataloging-in-Publication Data**
Gagne, Tammy.
 Using technology to find your family history / by Tammy Gagne.
   p. cm.—(A kid's guide to genealogy)
 Includes bibliographical references and index.
 ISBN 978-1-58415-951-3 (library bound)
 1. Genealogy—Juvenile literature. 2. Genealogy—Databases—Juvenile literature. 3. Genealogy—Computer network resources—Juvenile literature. I. Title.
 CS15.5.G34 2011
 929'.1072—dc22

                       2011000716

eBook ISBN: 9781612280943

                PLB

Contents

INTRODUCTION: CLIMBING THE FAMILY TREE

Learning about my family's history is one of my favorite pastimes. From interviewing family to finding documents that help me learn more, every step is fascinating. I think what makes this hobby the most fun is that it tells a story—my story. By researching your own family history, you can find your story.

Learning about your family history can be a little like traveling through time. Think of how it makes you feel when you listen to your parents and grandparents talk about the past. The more detail they provide, the more you feel like you were there with them, even if you hadn't been born yet. The same thing happens when you learn about your family tree. People whose names you might not have known at first suddenly become your ancestors, the people who made it possible for you to be here today.

You may begin looking into your family history because you are curious about a particular relative, or you might have to create a family tree for a school assignment. Oftentimes this glimpse into

the past leads to further research. The study of family history is called **genealogy.** This fun and informative hobby has never been more popular than it is today.

As you learn about your family's past, you also learn about yourself. You probably never met your second-great grandmother, but you just might find a photograph of her that helps explain where you got your dark, curly hair. Perhaps you and your father enjoy building things together. By studying your family history, you may discover that your third-great grandfather made his living as a carpenter. Both you and your dad may have inherited your fondness for working with your hands from this relative.

Genealogy also helps you learn about your heritage on a broader level. Maybe your ancestors lived in the colonies at the time of the American Revolution. Wouldn't it be exciting to find out that one of your relatives was a famous historical figure? Maybe you are among the seventh generation of your family to be

born in the United States. If so, where did your family live before one of them—or a bunch of them—came to the U.S.? How did they get here? Perhaps even more importantly, why did they come? Finding answers to questions like these is another exciting part of genealogy.

Technology has made genealogy research easier in many ways. Using email and instant messaging, you can ask questions and receive replies days or even weeks sooner than you could with traditional mail. Social networking sites like Facebook can connect you with long-lost relatives. Hundreds of sites contain data such as birth and marriage notices, court proceedings, and death certificates. Newspaper **archives** are also valuable resources that are free through many libraries. Some libraries even provide online access to their patrons from home. Someday microfiche and microfilm records will also be available online.

Always use common sense when going online. Get your parents' approval before registering at any site, whether it is free or not. Never contact anyone you don't know or provide your name or address without your parents' permission. Your mother and father may want to be involved in your genealogy project. If so, welcome their help. Part of the fun of genealogy is sharing what you find with the people you care about most.

St. Paul's Church in New York is a good example of the kind of church that also has an old cemetery to explore.

A librarian can show you how to use the library's computer programs for your genealogy research.

CHAPTER 1:
GETTING STARTED

Thanks to the Internet, beginning your search should be easy. A great deal of information is just a few clicks away if you have some basic information. Thousands of genealogy web sites with access to online databases are available. With the additional help of various public records, you may be able to assemble a family tree that includes many generations.

At one time people looking for the names of their ancestors had to visit multiple libraries and historical societies to track down information. This hands-on process took large amounts of time and effort. Today, genealogy is much less complicated, as long as you know where to start and how to use the information you find.

The Internet has made millions of useful records available to genealogists. This massive amount of information can overwhelm a beginner. Finding information may be a simple task, but finding the correct information can be much more challenging.

As tempting as it may be to start searching the databases right away, the smartest strategy is waiting just a bit. In fact don't even log on to your computer—yet. Instead, begin your genealogy project by recording all the information you already have. This data will be the foundation for your research, so it should be as complete as possible.

You may discover that one of your relatives received a Purple Heart in the military.

What Do You Know?

Your family tree begins with you. Other recent branches include your siblings, parents, aunts, uncles, cousins, and grandparents. Record each person's full name along with his or her date and place of birth. Most people also know at least a few facts about their great-grandparents and other extended family members. This could be as simple as your great-grandmother's name or that your great-grandfather was awarded a Purple Heart in World War II. You may not know a person's exact birth date, but just the year could be helpful. Also, be sure to record all maiden names, the last names of female family members prior to marriage. Maiden names are very important for researching the women in your family.

Talk to your parents and other family members to gather as much information as you can. Dates of birth, marriage, and death can be especially useful. Remember, different people may know different things. Some information you get may even conflict with other information. Your aunt might insist that your great grandmother's maiden name was Hill, but your cousin may be just as sure it was Bean. At this point you need not worry about accuracy. What matters most is recording every likely possibility. When it seems like you have hit a dead end, having alternate names to search can be extremely helpful.

When you do turn the computer on, begin by emailing other family members who may be able to give you more information. Email can be a practical way of communicating with family members who live far away. Tell them what you are doing, and ask if they would be willing to share any names, dates, or stories they know. You may find that some relatives have begun constructing family trees of their own, which could also be helpful to you.

It may be necessary to call or visit family members who don't use email. An in-person interview may be time consuming, but it can be one of your best resources. Older relatives often know a great deal about the past. A family reunion can be a great opportunity for interviewing numerous extended family members. If you don't have many older relatives who are still living, consider contacting your late relatives' friends and neighbors. They may be able to provide you with some of the basic information you are seeking. Don't forget to take along a pen and paper, but a digital recorder is a great way to make sure you don't overlook or misunderstand an important piece of information. Get each person's approval before recording your conversation.

Getting—And Staying—Organized

The most successful genealogists are organized ones. Even the best piece of information won't help you if you can't locate it when you need it. One of the best ways to keep your information organized is by storing it on your computer. Be sure to back up your records. Many subscription genealogy web sites allow users to keep their data online, but saving or printing important documents to keep at home is a smart step. If you cancel your subscription or your computer crashes, you don't want to lose all the names, dates, and sources you have collected.

You will also need to create a strategy for organizing all the new information you discover. There's a reason one's ancestry is called a family tree. All trees have numerous branches, which can lead the researcher in countless directions. Do you want to know more about your mother's family through her father's side or her mother's side? The path you choose to explore is up to you. By having a plan in place, you will be able to keep all your information straight.

You can purchase software that will help you list and source all the information you uncover. Some programs are designed for genealogists to organize their research. If you are especially good with computers, you could even create your own database for keeping and sorting your information. The program you find easiest to use is the best one for you.

One thing that will make your project easier is a file format called Genealogical Data Communication (GEDCOM). With GEDCOM, you can transfer data between different software programs. You can use it to share information with others, even if they have different software programs.

Queen Victoria's family tree gives you a good idea of just how many people from the past are connected to you.

Check and Cite Your Sources

Listening to family stories can be a great way to gather clues about your family's past. These stories can also be very entertaining. An important part of genealogy, however, is locating official documents to prove that the information in your family tree is accurate. Even if a family member provides you with a tree he or she has researched, always double-check the information, and keep track of the sources you've used.

You may be able to find photographs of some of your ancestors through the Internet. You can also upload photos of your own to some genealogy web sites.

CHAPTER 2:
START YOUR SEARCH ENGINES

When you go online to research a school report, the best place to start is a reliable search engine. The same thing is true for genealogical research. You can even begin your quest at a familiar site like Google. Search for the word *genealogy,* and you will find some of the most popular genealogy resources: The USGenWeb Project, Ancestry.com, and the National Archives, just to name a few. Smaller sites can be very helpful for finding details, but the best-known sites will provide the best general information.

The USGenWeb Project provides free information to genealogists. Volunteers work on national, state, and county levels to make as much information available as possible. This group's web site is a gateway to an ever-increasing number of smaller sites. These sites can provide a new genealogist with an amazing number of resources with no user fees.

Many other genealogy sites charge a monthly subscription fee. Longer commitments typically mean lower prices per month, but you must consider your options carefully. You don't want to subscribe to one site only to find that another one is much more thorough—or free. Many sites offer free trial periods, so you can test their search engines before deciding. Even if you feel certain in your choice, consider taking advantage of these trial offers. You may even spend a few weeks trying different sites before subscribing to any. Resist the urge to try too many at once, though. You may not have enough time to check out everything each site offers before your trial period runs out. For the same reason, be sure to collect as much basic information as possible before registering for a trial.

You may find a computer program that includes a subscription to a genealogy web site. Often, special television programs and genealogy blogs offer discounts for web subscriptions. Again, though, be selective, and always get your parents' permission. You don't want your inbox to become so flooded with blog updates that you miss other, more important messages—like a response from a newly discovered second cousin.

Some genealogy web sites offer a certain amount of free information before charging for their data. A new user may be allowed a particular number of searches for free, for example. Almost all sites charge for hard copies of original records, such as marriage and death certificates. Most often the information you view online will be summaries of the information contained in these documents.

Helpful Genealogy Web Sites

Free Sites	Subscription Sites
CastleGarden.org	Ancestry.com
DeadFred.com	Archives.com
DeathIndexes.com	Cyndislist.com
EllisIsland.org	Footnote.com
FamilySearch.org	GenealogyBank.com
FindAGrave.com	HistoryKat.com
National Archives (www.archives.gov)	NewspaperArchive.com
RootsWeb.ancestry.com	OneGreatFamily.com
SteveMorse.org	Origins.net
USGenWeb.org	WorldVitalRecords.com

You may want to order hard copies of important documents, like this marriage certificate from 1895.

A great way to search genealogy databases without having to pay a fee is accessing them through your local library. Many libraries have commercial subscriptions to sites such as Ancestry.com that patrons can use for free. State libraries and archives are often your best bets, but more and more smaller libraries are offering these services as well. One extremely helpful site, Heritage Quest Online, is available only to libraries.

Surprisingly, you may not have to visit your library to access its genealogy search engines. Some libraries allow patrons to log on from their home computers, using their library account information. You will still need to visit the library for certain pieces of information, but when you go, you can focus on the items you cannot access from home.

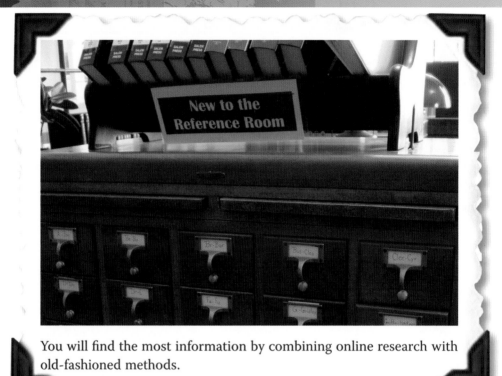

You will find the most information by combining online research with old-fashioned methods.

No matter how thorough any genealogy web site is, you won't be able to find everything you need in one place. Different sites will offer different advantages, and you may have to do some creative detective work for information that is especially hard to find.

Search Strategies

In addition to clues, a good detective needs good strategies. If your first search doesn't lead you to a relative, you will need to adjust your approach. For example, if you are having trouble getting results, try changing the spelling of the name you are searching. You may be certain that your great-grandfather spelled his name as Wendal. That doesn't mean, however, that his name wasn't recorded incorrectly on his draft card, which could provide you with his date of birth. Try searching his name as Wendel,

Wendall, or Wendell. It just might lead you to the information you seek.

Since early records were usually handwritten, many spelling mistakes were made when these documents were transcribed into typed form. Many old census forms are filled with elaborate penmanship, while others are extremely hard to read. Some information was undoubtedly recorded incorrectly on the original forms. A census taker may have recorded a man named Davis as David or a woman named Suzanne as Susan, simply from hearing the name wrong.

Sometimes nicknames can throw off a search. A man named William, for example, may also be found under the name Bill,

A census form from 1920. Census forms were filled out by hand and later typed into a national database. Errors were common.

If your relatives arrived on ships at Ellis Island, their names may have been changed at this time.

Billy, Will, Willy, or Liam. A woman named Elizabeth might be found under the name Beth, Libby, Lisa, Lizzie, or Lilibet. Remember, modern nicknames aren't always the same as ones used in years past. To find nicknames you may have overlooked, check a baby name web site. (Remember, sometimes you have to be creative!)

A person's heritage also could have affected the way his or her name was recorded. If the name of your Dutch ancestor was Joran, he may be listed as George (the English form of this name). Similarly, many last names were Americanized when **immigrants** entered the United States. A man with the last name Finkelstein may have shortened his name to Stein. Changes like this made it easier for many immigrants to find jobs. Other immigrants' names were changed based on their meanings. If your last name is Baker, you could have ancestors with the last name Becker, Boulanger, or Panettiere—the German, French, and Italian translations of this word.

Just like first names, last names too were often misspelled or transcribed incorrectly. If a person did not know how to read or write, the worker filling out the census form or immigration records had to decide how to spell that person's name. If a name was particularly difficult to say or spell, it may have been changed to make it simpler. A name like Papadopoulos, for example, may have been changed to Papas.

If you have an extremely common surname, finding your ancestors can be a bit like searching for a needle in a haystack. To narrow down your results, focus on relatives with unusual first names. There will be countless James Smiths on record, but there will be far fewer Japheth Smiths. Remember, though, just because a name isn't popular now, that doesn't mean it wasn't common long ago. You may be amazed by how many babies were named Japheth during the 1800s.

Other information that will improve your results include your ancestor's middle name; date of birth, marriage, and death; as well as places he or she lived. This is where all that information you collected in the beginning of your search will come in handy. Even a possible middle initial or birth year can cut hours of searching down to just seconds.

Once you have recorded all the information you have, check out Hamrick Software's surname distribution site. This resource can be extremely helpful for selecting a starting point for your searches. When you enter a last name along with a date, the results will tell you where most people with this name lived during that time period. You will have the best luck using this resource if your family's last name is an uncommon one.

Always begin your searches using the state only, even if you are absolutely certain that your relative lived in a particular town or city. Also, many search engines give users the option of entering a date range instead of a specific year. This may help you find your ancestor if a census record listed his or her date of birth as 1920 instead of 1919, for example.

Not everything you uncover will lead you to your relative, of course, but broad searches can increase the number of clues you collect.

Networking

Geography can pose some tough challenges to genealogists. Perhaps you would like to include a photo of your great-grandmother's childhood home in your project. If she lived in another state, this can be a difficult task. Maybe you are trying to track down her **obituary** to find her parents' names. Many larger newspapers publish their archives online, but some smaller ones don't. Instead of traveling hundreds of miles to dig up these

Your grandparents' childhood homes can yield hundreds of stories, like this one in Virginia did for the writer Earl Hamner Jr. Its stories inspired the 1970s television series *The Waltons.*

documents, you can ask a volunteer to help you.

Random Acts of Genealogical Kindness is a network of volunteers from every U.S. state and even some other countries. Each volunteer agrees to perform at least one search for a fellow genealogist each month, although some will do more. Visit their web site to read their guidelines. The USGenWeb Project offers a similar service. Because you are dealing with a volunteer, you won't need to pay the person to do the search for you. You will, however, need to repay the person for any fees he or she is charged, such as for photocopying. Also, you must not rely on this resource for information you can easily find on your own.

Always remember to thank the volunteer who helps you. Even a quick email to acknowledge the person's time and effort will be appreciated. Another great way to show your gratitude is by becoming a volunteer yourself. You probably won't end up helping the same person who helped you, but you can pay it forward by helping someone else.

Roots Television is an online resource with a twist. The site offers hundreds of free videos for genealogists. The content includes instructional programming as well as lectures from genealogy conferences. Users can watch the programs on their computers or stream them to their television sets. In addition to seeing videos made by professionals, users can also watch videos created by amateurs just like themselves. They can even upload their own videos to the site.

Census takers visited people across the country. Early censuses recorded little more than names and locations. Later censuses recorded ages, professions, and property information.

CHAPTER 3:
THE DOCUMENTS OF YOUR FAMILY HISTORY

One of the most useful documents used for genealogy research is the U.S. Census. As required by the U.S. Constitution, it is conducted every ten years. At first, the census only kept track of the country's population. By 1850, though, it was used to collect information on education, employment, housing, and more.

You can use the census to track where your ancestors were throughout their lives. You can also find out who lived in your ancestors' household and how old they were. A census record for your great-grandfather can lead you to the name of his parents, siblings, and other family members.

Census data about individuals cannot be released to the public until 72 years have passed since their collection. This rule was made to protect the privacy of people who are still alive. (Of course, people over the age of 72 who are still living will appear on the census forms that you can view now, but they would have been very young at the time.)

Today, census forms are printed electronically and mailed to every household in the United States. You might remember your parents filling out your household's census questionnaire in 2010. If they forgot to return their form, an **enumerator** may have visited your home. Enumerators travel door to door to collect the information and to help families fill out the form. The name of the enumerator for each census record is included on the document—information that many genealogists appreciate.

Each census has collected slightly different information. From 1790 to 1840, the census recorded only the names of heads of households. In 1850, however, the name of each resident was recorded. The 1860 census was much like the previous schedule, but the 1870 census stands out as the first year to include former **slaves** by name. In 1880, relationships were added. Unfortunately, most of the 1890 census records were destroyed in a fire.

The 1900 census is unique in that it can provide you with the birth month and year of your ancestor. This was also the first year that information about immigrants was collected. If you suspect

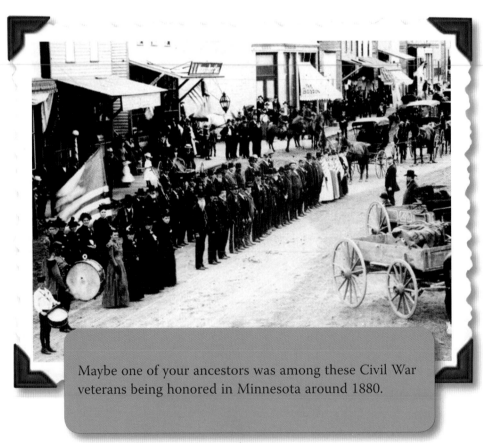

Maybe one of your ancestors was among these Civil War veterans being honored in Minnesota around 1880.

one of your ancestors was a Civil War veteran, the 1910 census may be able to confirm your hunch. The 1920 census won't tell you anything about your ancestor's military service, but it will tell you the language each household member spoke.

When searching U.S. Census records from 1880 to 1920, you may encounter a code called the **Soundex** system. This special way of indexing names can make it easier to find a name that was changed over time. Each name is represented by a letter and three numbers. Once you learn how to convert names into their Soundex codes, you will probably find it fairly easy. In the beginning, though, it can seem a bit complicated. For a simple converter program, visit RootsWeb's Soundex Converter.

Every Soundex code consists of four characters: a letter followed by three numbers. The letter is always the first letter of the surname. The numbers stand for the letters in the chart below. Vowels are only used as the first letter of the name. Likewise, the letters *h, w,* and *y* aren't used except at the beginning of a name. If a name has double consonants or a code has a repeating number, the second character is dropped. Extra letters are also dropped. Zeroes may be added if a name has only one or two letters that can be substituted with numbers.

Number	Represents the Letter
1	B, F, P, V
2	C, G, J, K, Q, S, X, Z
3	D, T
4	L
5	M, N
6	R

Here are a few examples of names and their Soundex codes:
Collins becomes C452.
Fowler becomes F460.
Hanson, Hansen, Hanssen, and Hansson each becomes H525.
Sumner becomes S560.

Many people consider the 1930 census the most interesting. It includes information about the value of each family's home, the amount of each family's rent or mortgage payment, and even whether someone in the household owned a radio. Remember, there were no computers or televisions in 1930. Radio was the latest technology, and owning a receiver was a sign of wealth in this era.

Several other nations have conducted their own census surveys, but each country has gone about the task a bit differently. Some of these documents can be useful to genealogists, while others are not. Census records may be helpful if you can trace your roots back to Austria, Canada, Italy, Norway, or the United Kingdom. Germany conducted a dozen censuses between 1871 and 1939, but these surveys collected statistical information only, no names. Australia has conducted a census every ten years since 1901. However, the law requires that the returns be destroyed after the government uses them.

Vital Records

Vital records are documents that record births, marriages, and deaths. Today the law requires the keeping of these records, but this has not always been the case. While some northern states recorded the births, marriages, and deaths of their residents as early as the seventeenth century, many other states did not. It wasn't until the twentieth century that the majority of states registered this important information.

When you can find them, birth certificates can be extremely helpful to your research. The typical information these documents include are the child's name, gender, and race; the date and place of birth; and the parents' names. Some states are protective of birth records. While census information is released publicly after 72 years, birth records may not be available for viewing until 100 years have passed. Again, the concern is privacy.

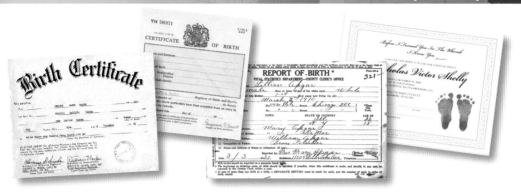

Marriage records are among the best sources for finding a woman's maiden name. Before two people can marry, they must apply for a marriage license. When they are wed, a marriage certificate documents the union. These records include the bride's name, the groom's name, and the place where the ceremony took place. Some records also specify birthplaces, occupations, names and birthplaces of the couple's parents, and information about previous marriages of either party.

Death records show when and where a person died. The best resources for finding death records are mortality schedules, DeathIndexes.com, and the Social Security Death Index. Which one will provide you with the information you need depends on when your relative died. Mortality schedules are included with the census records from 1850 to 1885. These specific censuses recorded the names of people who died the previous year. This information can be helpful, since few states used death certificates during this time period.

The best thing about finding a death record is that it can lead you to another, more detailed record: an obituary, or death announcement. Once you know a relative's date and place of death, you can then check the archives of local newspapers for this important news item. Obituaries include a wealth of information for genealogists. This simple write-up can provide you with information about your relative's birth date and place; parents, siblings, spouses, and children; his or her childhood years; his or her education and occupation; and places where he or she lived.

Many immigrants came to this country to pursue their dreams of owning land.

Land Records

Hundreds of years ago, the wealth of a family was measured mostly by the amount of land its members owned. Land records, or **deeds,** can tell you exactly where your relatives lived and how much property they owned. They can be especially helpful for ancestors who lived prior to 1790, when the U.S. Census began. Land records can also provide you with names of spouses, children, and other family members. Some records can even tell you where your ancestor lived before owning the land.

In order to find land records, you must have a general idea of where your ancestors lived. Most documents of this kind are kept locally. County clerks' offices and state archives will be most helpful. Deed transfers that were printed in newspapers can also provide you with useful information.

Today most property is purchased or inherited from relatives. In America's earliest years, however, there were other common ways of acquiring land. Your ancestors might have received property called **bounty lands** in exchange for military service or other work for the government. They may have gotten land through **homesteading.** The Homestead Act of 1862 made it possible for people to receive land at no upfront cost. Each homesteader received 160 acres of property in exchange for a promise to live on the land and farm it. At the end of five years, homesteaders who had built a house and farmed a certain portion of the land were given full ownership. If your ancestors received bounty lands or were homesteaders, your best resources for documentation are:

The Bureau of Land Management, The Official Federal Land Records Site, Eastern States Land Office (for land east of the Mississippi River)

The National Archives: Land Records (for land west of the Mississippi River)

Some of the documents that you may find useful when searching for land records include:

- Bounty land warrant applications
- Multiple grantor deeds, fractional deeds, and quitclaim deeds (good resources for information about children and places of family origin)
- Patents or first deeds (the earliest land record documents in the U.S.)
- Private land claims
- Property tax records

Other Records

If you are having trouble tracking down a birth certificate, consider looking for a slightly different type of document: a baptism record or a record of a person's bris milah (a Jewish ceremony for newborn boys) or other naming ceremony. The bris milah is given eight days after birth, so you can figure out a birth date from there. A baptism record may give you only the date of the child's

At the bris milah, a baby boy receives his Hebrew name. A girl may receive her Hebrew name during a Friday night (Shabbat) ceremony at temple, one week after her birth; or at home eight days after her birth in a ceremony called bris bat.

christening (instead of the exact birth date), but it will give you a rough idea of when he or she was born. Since many genealogy search engines allow you to search within a range of dates, this estimate can be helpful.

You might find records of baptism or other naming ceremonies at your ancestor's church or other place of worship, if it still exists. Many times when one church closes, its records are moved to a nearby parish of the same denomination. Sometimes, though, records are transferred to a local historical society.

Records from places of worship can also provide other types of information, such as marriages and funerals. You can also find burial information in the records of cemeteries, whether public or private. If you don't know the name of your ancestor's place of worship, don't despair. Another place to find information about baptisms, marriages, and burials is the newspaper.

Taking the Bad with the Good

Not everything you discover about your family's history will be pleasant. Perhaps one of your ancestors committed a terrible crime. You may be tempted to leave certain relatives off your tree for this reason, but I urge you not to do so. Some people refer to members of a family who get into trouble as black sheep. If you have a black sheep in your family tree, don't hide this important information. Not only is it okay to have a black sheep in your tree, but it can also make your project more interesting. A unique web site exists to celebrate people with the most despicable ancestors. Members of the International Black Sheep Society of Genealogists are descendants of murderers, thieves, political assassins, and other villains.

Greek emigrants prepare to row to a ship that will take them to the United States in 1910.

CHAPTER 4: CROSSING INTERNATIONAL BORDERS

Unless you are of purely Native American descent, if you live in the United States, researching your family history will eventually lead you to at least one other country. When this happens, many questions will arise: From which country or countries did your ancestors hail? When and how did they arrive in the United States? What records will prove their voyages?

People from Europe, Asia, and Africa began traveling to North America during the 1600s. The reasons were as different as the people themselves. Some were seeking adventure. Most came to build a better life for themselves and their families. War, religious persecution, and starvation in their homelands prompted many people to make their life-changing journeys. Some people willingly came as **indentured servants** in exchange for passage. Others were brought by force and sold as slaves.

Discovering when an ancestor crossed an ocean to get to the United States can be one of the most exciting finds in your research. It can also be one of the most challenging. During the early nineteenth century, ships were not required to keep passenger lists. Also, if your ancestor had an especially common name, it may take you a while to locate the correct documents.

Middle names were not used in the 1800s as often as they are today. You may know that your fifth-great grandfather was named David Littlefield, but you may not know how popular this name was in England more than 200 years ago. Without a distinctive middle name, you will have to sift through many documents before finding the David Littlefield who married your fifth-great grandmother on American soil.

The best way to begin your search for a foreign ancestor is starting with what you already know. If your grandmother told you that your family came from Scotland, ask her if she knows which region of this country your ancestors called home. Simply knowing that your ancestors lived in the Highlands or the Lowlands can be helpful. Also, make note of any unusual names—of people or places. The more unique the name, the more quickly you will be able to find it.

You also must be certain that your relative was indeed an immigrant. Sometimes families believe that a particular ancestor was born in another country when he or she was actually the grandson or granddaughter of the true immigrant. To help avoid this common mistake, be sure to check all domestic records for

Perhaps one of your ancestors lived in a house like this one in the Scottish Highlands.

your ancestor before moving on to immigration records.

Once you are confident that the ancestor you seek was an immigrant, you can then look for passenger lists and **naturalization** papers.

Passenger Lists

In 1819, the U.S. government passed a law requiring all ship captains to file a list of passengers for each voyage with the **customs department.** These early passenger lists are available at the National Archives' web site. They include the names, ages, genders, occupations, and countries of origin of all the passengers on the ship. Each list also includes the name of the vessel and its captain, the point from which the ship sailed, and the date and port of its arrival in the United States.

As more and more people immigrated, more and more information was recorded. In 1903, captains began recording the race of each passenger. In 1906, they began including a description of each passenger, along with his or her birthplace. In 1907, the largest number of immigrants to date arrived in the United States—over 1.5 million people. This was also the year that passenger lists began including the name and address of each person's nearest relative in his or her home country.

Names on a ship's passenger list from 1878

Naturalization Papers

If your ancestor became a U.S. citizen, you may be able to find a record of this event. Also called naturalization, the process of becoming a citizen at this time involved filling out a form, which was filed at the local courthouse. The Internet has made locating documents like these easier, but many of these types of records are still waiting to be entered into a national database. One of the best places to start searching for naturalization records is Ancestry.com.

Finding African Ancestors

If your ancestors came to the United States from Africa, you will use the same tools as genealogists of other ethnic backgrounds—to a point. Once you trace your family tree back to about 1870, your work may become more challenging. Don't be discouraged by this. Your resources for information may be more limited, but they aren't nonexistent. Many Africans were taken to the Caribbean before coming to the United States. The Barbados Slave Registers or CaribbeanRoots.com may be helpful if your ancestors were among this group of people.

Most African people who came to the United States before the Civil War were forced to immigrate and become slaves. Although U.S. census records include slave schedules, these may not be your best bet in finding detailed information about your ancestor. The law did not require enumerators to record the names of slaves. Try searching for these records of the slave owner instead:

- probate records
- tax records
- plantation records
- Freedman's Bureau records
- runaway slave records

One of the kids in this photograph, taken in Pennsylvania in 1898, could be your second or third great-grandparent.

Many slaves served in the Civil War. If your ancestor was one of them, you may be able to find information from military records as well. Visit the Civil War Soldiers and Sailors System to begin your search.

The Pitfalls of International Research
As your research shifts to a foreign country, the language barrier may present a challenge. Your ancestors may have come to the United States from Mexico, but this doesn't mean that you or anyone close to you speaks or reads Spanish. In this case, translation tools such as Google Translation, Babel Fish, or Free Translation Services may be helpful.

When you are researching a new country, it may feel as if you are starting from the very beginning. The types of records kept in that country and how you access them can be very different from the documents and procedures in the United States. Many genealogy web sites offer subscription upgrades for tracking down foreign documents, but before you take that route, you may want to do some basic research on your country of origin.

Learning about the history and geography of the country could also prove to be very helpful. For instance, the boundaries of many countries have changed over time. Some have changed more than once. For this important reason, your search could lead you to neighboring countries as well.

True Technology at Work

If your search goes cold before you discover an ancestor from another country, you might worry that you will never know where your international origins lie. Don't give up just yet! **Molecular genealogy** may be able to answer the questions that neither family members nor painstaking research can.

Believe it or not, you carry the most important clue to your ancestry with you wherever you go. Your **deoxyribonucleic acid,** better known as DNA, can help you discover which part of the world your ancestors called home. Since we inherit DNA from our parents, it can be used to identify the unique combination of ethnic groups to which you belong. The same type of cheek swab you've probably seen used in crime scene television programs can provide genealogists with important information about ancestry.

If your ancestors sailed to the United States from another country, this view may have been their first glimpse of America. The Statue of Liberty has welcomed many immigrants to the United States.

DNA is a string of codes found in the nucleus of every living cell. It contains information such as eye color, skin tone, and other physical traits, as well as traits having to do with mental and physical ability. Since a person's DNA comes from his or her parents, it can be used to trace the person's ancestry.

For more information, visit the International Society of Genetic Genealogy on the web.

Even with advancing technology, an accurate family history project can take years to piece together. Getting your facts right is essential, but learning the stories behind the facts is part of what makes genealogy fun. Another thrilling aspect of genealogy is often the search itself. You may find yourself feeling sad that your search is over when you have uncovered your last family record. If you do, remember that another part of genealogy is sharing what you have discovered with other family members. They will probably be just as fascinated by the information as you have been. By mapping your family history, you create a wonderful resource that you can pass down to future generations. Remember, you too will probably be someone's ancestor someday.

A Trip to the Past
The most common immigration site of the twentieth century was Ellis Island, located near the tip of New York City. More than 12 million immigrants passed through Ellis Island during the 62 years it was open. If your ancestor was one of them, you may want to visit this site. The Ellis Island Immigration Museum is part of the Statue of Liberty National Monument. The museum offers visitors a 45-minute tour that allows them to relive the experience of their ancestors when they entered the United States. The tour is available in nine different languages.

FURTHER READING

BOOKS

Beller, Susan Provost. *Roots for Kids: A Genealogy Guide for Young People.* Baltimore, Maryland: Genealogical Publishing Company, 2010.

Crowe, Elizabeth. *Genealogy Online.* San Francisco, California: McGraw-Hill Osborne Media, 2009.

Dollarhide, William. *Getting Started in Genealogy Online.* Baltimore, Maryland: Genealogical Publishing Company, 2009.

Morgan, George G. *The Official Guide to Ancestry.com.* Provo, Utah: Ancestry.com, 2008.

WORKS CONSULTED

Helm, Matthew L., and April Leigh. *Online Genealogy for Dummies.* Hoboken, New Jersey: Wiley, 2008.

Morgan, George G. *How to Do Everything Genealogy.* New York: McGraw-Hill Osborne Media, 2009.

———. *The Official Guide to Ancestry.com.* Provo, Utah: Ancestry.com, 2008.

Powell, Kimberly. *The Everything Guide to Online Genealogy.* Avon, Massachusetts: Adams Media, 2008.

Smolenyak, Megan. *Who Do You Think You Are? The Essential Guide to Tracing Your Family History.* New York: Viking Adult, 2010.

ON THE INTERNET

Ancestry.com
http://www.ancestry.com
Barbados Slave Registers
http://landing.ancestry.co.uk/intl/uk/barbados.aspx
Bureau of Land Management, The Official Federal Land Records Site, Eastern States Land Office (for land east of the Mississippi River)
http://www.glorecords.blm.gov/
CaribbeanRoots.com
http://www.caribbeanroots.com/
Civil War Soldiers and Sailors System
http://www.itd.nps.gov/cwss/
Family Tree of the Jewish People
http://www.jewishgen.org/
Free Translation Services
http://www.freetranslation.com/

Google Translation
    http://translate.google.com
Hamrick Software: U.S. Surname Distribution
    http://hamrick.com/names/
International Black Sheep Society of Genealogists
    http://www.ibssg.org/blacksheep/
International Society of Genetic Genealogy
    http://www.isogg.org/
National Archives: Land Records
    http://www.archives.gov/research/land/
National Archives: Resources for Genealogists
    http://www.archives.gov/research/genealogy/
Online Searchable Death Indexes & Records
    http://www.deathindexes.com/
Random Acts of Genealogical Kindness
    http://www.raogk.org/
Roots Television: Free Genealogy, Family History Videos
    http://www.rootstelevision.com/
RootsWeb's Soundex Converter
    http://resources.rootsweb.ancestry.com/cgi-bin/soundexconverter
Social Security Death Index
    http://www.genealogybank.com/gbnk/ssdi/
U.S. Census Bureau
    http://www.census.gov/
USGenWeb Project
    http://usgenweb.org/
U.S. Virgin Islands Vital Records
    http://genealogy.about.com/library/vital/blvirginislands.htm
Yahoo! Babel Fish
    http://babelfish.yahoo.com/

archives (AR-kyvs)—A place where public records or other historical documents are kept.

bounty lands (BOWN-tee LANDZ)—Areas of property given to early U.S. citizens in exchange for military service or other government work.

customs department (KUS-tumz deh-PART-munt)—A federal law enforcement agency responsible for trade and immigration.

deed (DEED)—A document that proves property ownership.

deoxyribonucleic acid (dee-OK-see-ry-boh-noo-KLAY-ik AS-id)—The main component of chromosomes that deliver genetic characteristics (such as hair and eye color); also called DNA.

enumerator (ee-NOO-muh-ray-tor)—Someone who counts or makes lists of things, such as a census taker.

genealogy (jee-nee-OL-uh-jee; *also,* jee-nee-AL-uh-jee)—The study of family history.

homestead (HOHM-sted)—Land, with the buildings on it, that is earned by living on and farming it.

immigrant (IH-muh-grunt)—A person who moves into a country from another country.

indentured servant (in-DEN-cherd SUR-vunt)—A person who agreed to work for an employer for a fixed period of time in exchange for passage to North America.

molecular genealogy (moh-LEK-yuh-ler jee-nee-OL-uh-jee)—The practice of using DNA to find out where a person's family is originally from.

naturalization (nat-cheh-ruh-lih-ZAY-shun)—The process of becoming a citizen of a country.

obituary (oh-BIT-choo-ayr-ee)—A detailed death notice, usually appearing in a newspaper.

slave (SLAYV)—A person who is considered to be the property of another person.

Soundex (SOWN-dex)—A code system created in the 1930s that is used to simplify names in census records.

INDEX

ABOUT THE
AUTHOR

Tammy Gagne is the author of numerous books for adults and children, including My Guide to the Constitution: *The Power of the States* for Mitchell Lane Publishers. She is an avid genealogist who has traced her own family history all the way to Hampshire, England, circa 1500. She resides in northern New England with her husband and son. One of her favorite pastimes is visiting schools to speak to kids about the writing process.